SACRED

SATB (with divisions) *a cappella*

OXFORD

JOHN RUTTER
OPEN THOU MINE EYES

ANNIVERSARY · EDITION

Composer's note

This brief *a cappella* anthem (suitable as an introit or call to worship) was written in 1980 at the invitation of the Texas Choral Directors Association as one of a set of three, the other two being *For the beauty of the earth* and *Lord, make me an instrument of thy peace*.

The author of the text, Lancelot Andrewes, was an Anglican clergyman and scholar who held important posts as Master of Pembroke College, Cambridge (1589–1605), Bishop of Chichester (1605–9), of Ely (1609–18), and of Winchester (1618–26). He was renowned in his own day for his sermons—he often preached before King James I—but is remembered now chiefly as one of the team of translators of the King James Bible; he acted as general editor, and it is said that he was responsible for more of the translation than any other scholar. The beauty of his English prose has been praised by writers as diverse as T. S. Eliot and Kurt Vonnegut, but, curiously, the lovely prayer *Open thou mine eyes* was originally written in Latin, as part of a collection of prayers, the *Preces privatae*, which was intended only for Andrewes's private use and not published until after his death in 1626. Many of these prayers are biblical paraphrases or compilations, often cast in a repetitive litany-like form. The English translation used in my musical setting was published in 1896 as part of an English edition of the *Preces privatae*, and is by Andrewes's first biographer, the 19th-century Scottish minister Alexander Whyte.

Performance hints

The melodic style of the music was inspired by the contours of Celtic folk-song, and it should be performed with a sense of freedom, fluidity, and gentle reflectiveness. The triplets should never feel hurried.

The humming (starting in bar 33) may be on an '*mm*' sound, an '*nn*' sound, or an '*ng*' sound (as in the end of the word 'thing'), whichever achieves the best balance with the solo line.

If preferred, the piece may be sung a semitone higher, in F sharp major.

Reproduction in concert programmes of the above composer's note (though not the performance hints) is permitted, subject to the following acknowledgement being printed:
'By John Rutter, © Oxford University Press 2014. Reproduced by permission of Oxford University Press.'

Commissioned by the Texas Choral Directors Association

Open thou mine eyes

Lancelot Andrewes (1555–1626)
trans. Alexander Whyte (1836–1921)

JOHN RUTTER

Flowing and reflective; rather freely ♩ = c. 63

O - pen thou mine eyes and I shall see: In-cline my heart and I shall de-sire: Or-der my steps and I shall walk In the ways of thy com-mand-ments.

O - pen thou mine eyes and I shall see: In-cline my heart and I shall de-sire:

O - pen thou mine eyes and I shall see: In-cline my heart and I shall de-sire:

Or-der my steps and I shall walk In the ways of thy com-

Or-der my steps and I shall walk In the ways of thy com-

© Oxford University Press 1980. This edition © 2014

Printed in Great Britain

OXFORD UNIVERSITY PRESS MUSIC DEPARTMENT, GREAT CLARENDON STREET, OXFORD OX2 6DP
The Moral Rights of the Composer have been asserted. Photocopying this copyright material is ILLEGAL.

18
S.
A.
T.
B.
p
- mand - ments.
mp dolce
O Lord God, be thou to me a God And be -
cresc.
O Lord God, be thou to me a God And be -
21
mf
- side thee let there be none else, No oth - er, naught else with
mp
- side thee let there be none else, No oth - er, naught else with

24
p legato
cresc.
Vouch-safe to me to wor-ship thee and serve thee Ac-cord-ing
p legato
cresc.
Vouch-safe to me to wor-ship thee and serve thee Ac-cord-ing
p
cresc.
thee. to wor-ship thee and serve thee Ac-cord-ing
p
cresc.
thee. to wor-ship thee and serve thee Ac-cord-ing
p
legato
cresc.
27
mp cresc.
to thy com-mand-ments, In truth of spi-rit, In rev-'rence of
mp cresc.
to thy com-mand-ments, In truth of spi-rit, In rev-'rence of
mp cresc.
to thy com-mand-ments, In truth of spi-rit, In rev-'rence of
mp cresc.
to thy com-mand-ments, In truth of spi-rit, In rev-'rence of
mp cresc.

bo-dy, In bless-ing of lips, In pri-vate and in pub-lic.

bo-dy, In bless-ing of lips, In pri-vate and pub-lic.

bo-dy, In bless-ing of lips, In pri-vate and pub-lic.

bo-dy, In bless-ing of lips, In pri-vate and pub-lic.

SOPRANO SOLO
(or SEMI-CHORUS)

O-pen thou mine eyes and I shall see: In-cline my heart and I shall de-

Hum

Hum

Hum

Hum

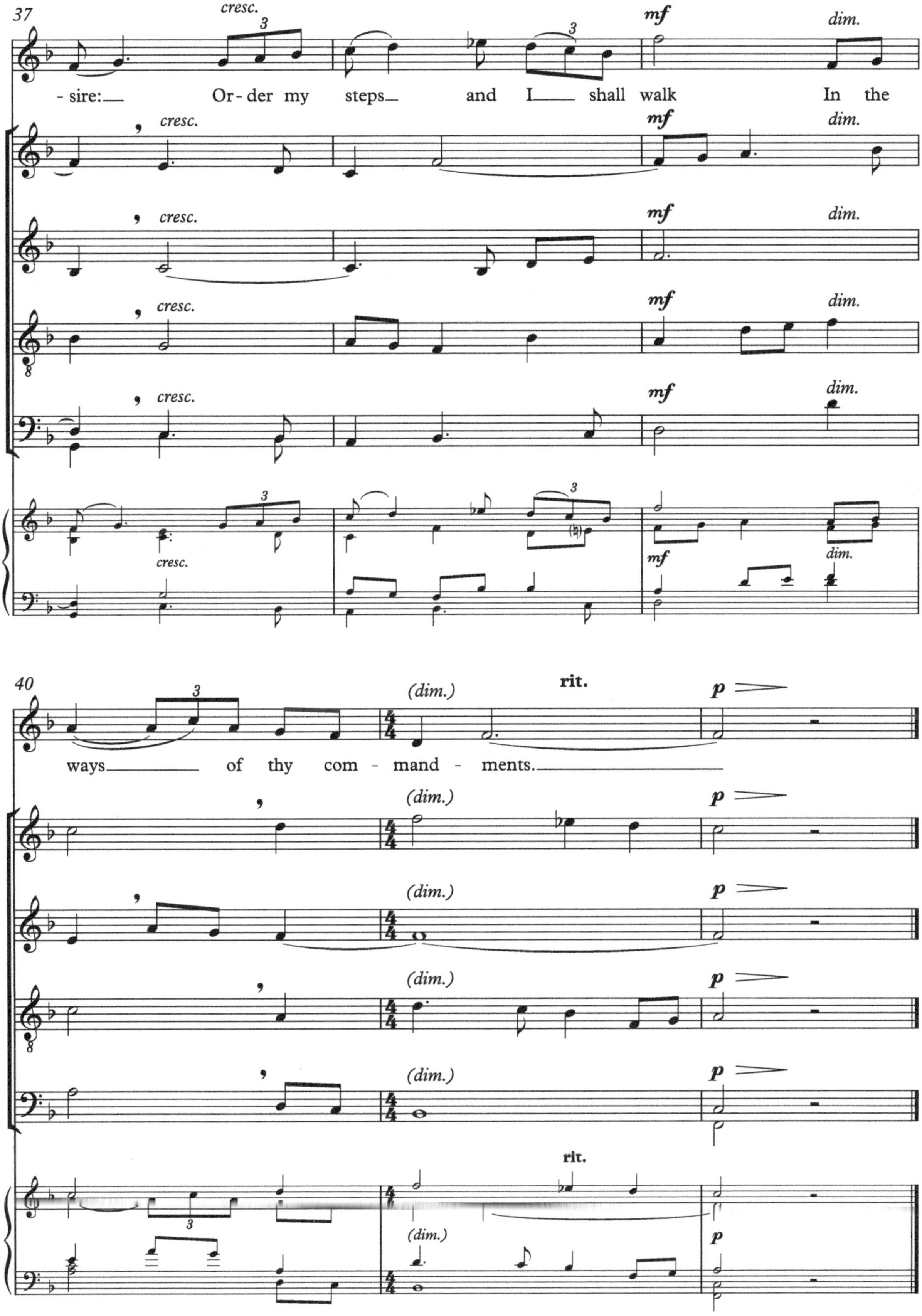

Printed by Halstan

The **John Rutter Anniversary Edition** celebrates the 70th birthday of one of Britain's leading composers and the 30th anniversary of his choir, The Cambridge Singers. Featuring mainly earlier pieces from the composer's catalogue, this series presents seminal works for mixed chorus in brand new editions and with accompanying notes on both the music and performance, written by the composer himself. The Anniversary Edition provides the most comprehensive and authoritative performance materials (including full scores and parts) for over 30 of the composer's favourite anthems, carols, and songs.

John Rutter CBE was born in London in 1945 and studied music at Clare College, Cambridge. His compositions embrace choral, orchestral, and instrumental music, and he has edited or co-edited various choral anthologies including four *Carols for Choirs* volumes with Sir David Willcocks and the *Oxford Choral Classics* series. He now divides his time between composition and conducting and is sought after as a guest conductor for the world's leading choirs and orchestras.

For more details about John Rutter and his music, please contact Oxford University Press, Music Department.

OXFORD
UNIVERSITY PRESS

www.oup.com

ISBN 978-0-19-340550-9